Worship

Biblical Truth Simply Explained

Baptism in the Holy Spirit
Jack Hayford

Biblical Meditation
Campbell McAlpine

Blessings and Curses
Derek Prince

Deliverance
Bishop Graham Dow

Forgiveness
John Arnott

The Holy Spirit
Dr. Bob Gordon

Prayer
Joyce Huggett

Rejection
Steve Hepden

Spiritual Protection
Lance Lambert

The Trinity
Jack Hayford

Trust
Tom Marshall

Worship
Jack Hayford

Worship

Jack Hayford

Chosen Books
A Division of Baker Book House Co
Grand Rapids, Michigan 49516

© 1996, 2003 by Jack Hayford

Published in the USA in 2003 by Chosen Books
a division of Baker Book House Company
P.O. Box 6287, Grand Rapids, MI 49516-6287
www.bakerbooks.com

Originally published under the title *Explaining Worship* by Sovereign
World Limited of Tonbridge, Kent, England

Printed in the United States of America

Library of Congress Cataloging-in-Publication Data
Hayford, Jack W.
[Explaining worship]
Worship / Jack Hayford.
p. cm. — (Biblical truth simply explained)
Originally published: Explaining worship. Tonbridge, Kent, England :
Sovereign World, 1996.
ISBN 0-8007-9352-8
1. Worship. I. Title. II. Series.

BV10.3.H39 2003
248.3—dc21
                                                    2003053179

Notes for study leaders

This book is intended to be instructive on all aspects of the topic of worship. It is also intended to challenge each reader about his or her personal attitudes toward worship and his or her practice of worship. Don't be surprised if strong reactions arise during the study, particularly when answering certain questions.

As a leader you will need to balance the needs of individuals with those of the whole group. It is best to model an accepting attitude to different opinions and responses. At the same time it is wise to not get sidetracked into devoting too much time to any one person's thoughts, but to enable everyone in the group to share and to respond to the positive thrust of the book.

Our hope is that as people think and pray through the subject of worship, their understanding will increase and worship will be released more fully in all areas of their lives. In some cases people will need to take practical steps in response to what is taught. It will help if the study takes place in an encouraging and receptive atmosphere where group members feel able to share honestly.

Encourage group members to read one chapter prior to each meeting and think about the issues in advance. It is usually good to review the content of the particular chapter at the meeting, however, to refresh everyone's memory and so that those who have not managed to "do their homework" will not feel embarrassed.

Five study questions at the end of each chapter will stimulate thought and encourage each person to consider how any of these issues may affect him or her personally. Praying together, asking for God's help, will help you to take hold of the truths presented.

May God bless you as you study this material yourself and lead others in doing so.

Contents

Introduction

Worship is our primary ministry. This is a fundamental truth. Reading the Bible, service and witnessing to others about Christ are extremely important. But our ministry to the Lord through worship is what brings life and freshness to all those other aspects of our walk with the Lord.

In this book we will look at many different aspects of worship and see that worship actually begins to aid in shaping us into God's image. Then, as we become conformed to His image, our ministry to others is a natural result.

1

The Meaning of Worship

In a tropical jungle a man bows before a crude stick figure; in a fantastic Asian temple another burns incense before a richly decorated Buddha. A small group of people meets in an unobtrusive house in a small town to sing and pray together. A man in an affluent suburb spends the entire morning meticulously washing and waxing his foreign-made sports car. A teenage girl listens adoringly to her favorite rock star in her poster-plastered bedroom.

All of these people are worshiping. In some cases, the worship is formal and easy to recognize. In others, most people would hesitate to call it worship at all. But everyone worships something or someone, and what you worship has a great influence on what you are.

In this chapter we will define worship and look at its meaning and importance. We will also come to see how worship shapes and guides our lives.

Defining worship

Human beings were made to worship. Whether they acknowledge it or not, everyone worships in one way or another. Some people worship their job, some worship money and some worship possessions. Some people worship a movie or television star, or a recording star; they even call him or her their "idol." Some people worship a goal or desire, some worship their own self-image, some worship pleasure and some worship God.

Although everyone worships something, many people don't even recognize what they are worshiping. Until we understand the meaning of worship, we'll never understand its purpose. And until we understand the wise principles of worship, we are in danger of violating them.

Worship comes from the Old-English word *weorthscipe* and means "to ascribe worth to." It contains the essential idea that we worship whatever we value most highly. Although people worship many things, worship rightly belongs to God. No one else can lay claim to the position of highest value in anyone's life.

The shaping influence of worship

Psalm 115 makes a very insightful statement on the subject of worship:

> Their idols are silver and gold,
>   made by the hands of men.
> They have mouths, but cannot speak,
>   eyes, but they cannot see;
> they have ears, but cannot hear,
>   noses, but they cannot smell;
> they have hands, but cannot feel,
>   feet, but they cannot walk;
>   nor can they utter a sound with their throats.
> Those who make them will be like them,
>   and so will all who trust in them.
>
> Psalm 115:4–8

In this passage the psalmist is talking about idolatry and the inadequacy of the idol gods that the heathen were worshiping. Then he makes a very important statement: "Those who make them will be like them, and so will all who trust in them." In other words, the Bible says that you become like the god you worship. Let me say it again: *You become like the god you worship.* By the influence of worship, the entire direction of your life is established.

Worship means you are determining values; you are deciding what you desire the most. You are fixing priorities and establishing what holds first place in your life. Worship means you are shaping what you are going to become; you are choosing in what image you will be made.

The psalmist observes a historically verifiable fact: People become like what they worship. The gods that are worshiped begin to manifest their attributes in the worshiper. So in worship you are making decisions about your values, your priorities and what you will ultimately become.

The issue of worship: determining your life's direction

Since worship sets your values and priorities, it will consequently determine the outflow of your life. It will affect *what* you seek and *where* you seek it. That will in turn determine what you discover and the kind of fulfillment you will achieve.

J. B. Phillips said there is a God-shaped vacuum in every one of us, which only God can fill. Worship is the way we fill that place. So when we worship with wisdom, we become like the Lord with whom we're filling our inner life.

Augustine expressed it like this: "Lord, you've made us for yourself, and our hearts find no rest until they find it in you." We were created for God, and the fulfillment of our hearts comes as a direct result of us approaching Him and coming to know Him.

So some very significant issues are determined by our worship. In worship we determine where we're going to bow. By bowing, I don't just mean a physical posture, but a stance of the soul.

Worship has to do with whom we seek and to whom we submit. The goal that we press toward becomes the guiding force of our lives. We bring our hearts into alignment with whatever we worship, so they begin to mirror the object of our worship.

Worship determines what we will discover. Those who seek the Lord will discover the true purpose for which we were made, and its fulfillment. Those who follow other gods will discover what those gods provide, whether it be worry and care, decadence, poverty or emptiness. Ultimately, there is no other fulfillment for that God-shaped place in us than the Lord Himself.

Finally, our worship determines what flows from our lives. Our highest attainment comes through glorifying Him who is worthy of all glory. Others may find some temporary glory in their works or pursuits. Some may even be remembered beyond their lifetime. But those who worship the Lord, looking to the unseen rather than to the seen, will find what Paul calls an "eternal weight of glory" (2 Corinthians 4:17, KJV) working in their lives. Despite the trials of this life, they will have a glory that endures.

God reveals Himself to those who bow before Him and seek Him. If we truly seek Him with all our hearts, we'll find Him. Then, when we discover what He's really like, glorifying Him becomes the natural result. The most logical response in the universe to meeting God is to want to glorify Him, and worship leads us along that path.

Study questions:
1. What does the author mean when he says that "everyone worships something or someone"?
2. What do the origins of the word *worship* tell us about its meaning?
3. How is it that we "become like the god we worship"?
4. In what way does worship determine our life's direction?
5. Who or what are you worshiping?

2

The Call to Worship

One of my most vivid memories of my first trip to Jerusalem was being awakened very early in the morning by the blaring speakers of a nearby mosque. The *muezzin* was calling the Muslims to worship.

That is a well-known modern example of a call to worship, but we are going to study another call to worship associated with the same location where I was startled out of sleep. In Jerusalem is one of Islam's holiest sights: the Dome of the Rock. That building was constructed over the location where Muslims believe Abraham went to sacrifice Isaac. It is that incident that we will study in this chapter.

This chapter will help us understand God's call to Abraham and how it relates to us today. It will teach about both the demands and the blessings of the call to worship.

Abraham's trial

One of the most extraordinary stories in the Bible has to do with worship. The key verse that introduces this story is Genesis 22:1–2.

> Some time later God tested Abraham. He said to him, "Abraham!"
> "Here I am," he replied.
> Then God said, "Take your son, your only son, Isaac, whom you love, and go to the region of Moriah. Sacrifice him there as a burnt offering on one of the mountains I will tell you about."

Abraham received a call to worship. But what a shocking call it was! Can you imagine what Abraham must have thought and felt? "The God of love whom I serve, who has called me from the emptiness of a world that kills its young, is now commanding me to take my only son and sacrifice him." And yet that was God's call.

In every one of our lives, there is a call to worship much like Abraham's. The call to worship that he received, alien as it seems, has a very real application to us. But to understand it, we need to look at the whole story.

The Lord called Abraham to sacrifice his son. That sounds hideous, doesn't it? It seemed a perversion of God's nature as Abraham understood it and as God's nature truly is. But Abraham followed the Lord, notwithstanding what seemed to be a tormenting vision of his only son slain on a pile of wood and going up in flames.

Abraham's answer to the call brought him to a place called Moriah, where God directed that he go and offer the sacrifice.

> When they reached the place God had told him about, Abraham built an altar there and arranged the wood on it. He bound his son Isaac and laid him on the altar, on top of the wood. Then he reached out his hand and took the knife to slay his son. But the angel of the Lord called out to him from heaven, "Abraham! Abraham!"
>
> "Here I am," he replied.
>
> "Do not lay a hand on the boy," he said. "Do not do anything to him. Now I know that you fear God, because you have not withheld from me your son, your only son."
>
> Genesis 22:9–12

The Bible tells us that the Lord provided another sacrifice, for Abraham turned and saw a ram caught by his horns in a thicket, and he offered the ram in place of Isaac. And in the New Testament we read that Abraham was so persuaded about the faithful nature of God that he believed that if he did slay Isaac, God would raise him from the dead (Hebrews 11:17–19).

Abraham is called the father of the faith. And this faith is that of those who answer God's call to worship.

The demands of worship

As it was with Abraham, so it is with us. If we answer God's call to worship, there are certain things that will be required of us.

The first is that we'll be called to a new place with Him. The Lord said, "Go to the place I will tell you about." God calls us to a new place in following Him, by responding to His call to worship Him in a way we've never learned before.

Secondly, we are called to surrender to God's claims. The Lord said, "Sacrifice your only son." Just as Isaac was the product of Abraham and Sarah's bodies, there are things in our lives that are our "children." Perhaps it's a project or goal we wish to accomplish, our aspirations for the future. It may be our actual children, or dreams we have for them. It may be attitudes about our rights in this life. Many times the Lord will call us to surrender those things that are at the heart of our aspirations and dreams.

"Will you lay them on the altar before me?" God asks, and we are full of fear.

"But, God, if I do that, I'll lose what I'm all about."

If we press on, we always discover that His true nature is never to destroy what He created us to be, but rather to release in us what has always been His highest intention.

This is how it was with Abraham. Through risking the loss of Isaac, believing that God was able to resurrect even the child lying dead, he discovered that God's will was not to take his son's life. Instead, God's will was to take away Abraham's fears. It resulted in a fresh revelation of God's nature: His goodness, mercy and grace.

The blessings of worship

Abraham saw a new facet of the nature of God, and he called that place Jehovah-Jireh: The Lord will provide. Just as Abraham's obedience resulted in a new revelation of God's person and purpose, so our call to worship brings us to fresh discovery and a further disclosure of God's nature and His high provision.

As we come in worship, we find God's nature revealed in fresh, new ways. God calls us to worship not to exploit us, but to expose our fears and remove them. And as we answer that call, we are introduced to the discovery of our "very great reward" (Genesis 15:1). That's why we're called to walk in the steps of Abraham.

Abraham's reward went way beyond the provision of the ram. Genesis 22:15–18 tells us that the Lord blessed Abraham in response to his faithfulness. We, likewise, find that we are blessed in response to answering the call to worship. The very things that we were afraid of losing are often the things that the Lord promises to multiply and bless abundantly.

Study questions:

1. How was God's command for Abraham to sacrifice Isaac a call to worship?
2. What does that story tell us about God's nature?
3. What are two demands that worship places upon us?
4. What are two blessings that come from worship?
5. In what ways have you personally heard and responded to that call to worship?

3

The God We Worship

In the earlier studies, we talked about the meaning and significance of worship. We have seen how God calls us to come and worship Him, that we might be transformed into His image.

But what is that image? What is the God we worship really like? That's a very important issue, for if as the Bible says we become like the one we worship, then it's important to worship the Lord as He truly is, rather than as some figment of our imagination.

That is one of the reasons for the gift of the Scriptures, that we might have a revelation of God's true nature. In this chapter we will see just what Scripture says about the nature of God.

In this chapter we will study an example of worship based on who God is and explain five key attributes of God— that He is *eternal, almighty, omnipresent, all-knowing* and *holy*. It will help us to know more of the traits of the Lord and to understand what is meant by the phrase, "magnify the Lord."

David's worship

In 1 Chronicles 29, David gave a tremendous example of praise based on the character of God. A great offering had been given toward the Temple that Solomon was to build, and now David dedicated this to the Lord and gave thanks. He began with a stirring recitation of the magnificence of the Lord.

Let's read about the God we worship:

David praised the LORD in the presence of the whole assembly, saying,

> "Praise be to you, O LORD,
>   God of our father Israel,
>   from everlasting to everlasting.
> Yours, O LORD, is the greatness and the power
>   and the glory and the majesty and the splendor,
>   for everything in heaven and earth is yours.
> Yours, O LORD, is the kingdom;
>   you are exalted as head over all.
> Wealth and honor come from you;
>   you are the ruler of all things.
> In your hands are strength and power
>   to exalt and give strength to all.
> Now, our God, we give you thanks,
>   and praise your glorious name."
>
> 1 Chronicles 29:10–13

In those few verses there are no less than twelve statements glorifying God, and each one of them says something significant about the God we worship.

David begins by saying, "Yours, O LORD, is the greatness." In that statement he declares that magnificence and majesty are due the Lord. In other words, our worship rightfully belongs to God.

David continues naming other things that belong to God: "the power and the glory and the majesty." He is not just rattling off words; each of these expressions has significance. *Power* refers to the strength that God has to accomplish things in the physical dimension. *Glory* signifies the splendid brightness of His presence, the *shekinah* glory of God.

The term *majesty* means sincerity, truth, confidence, perfection and completeness. It has also been translated "victory," and if you think of someone guaranteeing victory for your side, that means he or she is going all out to win. You can be confident that he or she is 100 percent behind you. Furthermore, he or she will continue to press forward on your behalf until victory is completed and perfected. That is good reason to praise God! The victory is His.

Splendor expresses the exalted position of eminence and beauty that the Lord holds. David closes the verse by saying that God is the possessor of everything. As the Creator, He is also the rightful owner. Everything belongs to Him!

David continues by declaring that God rules over all and that everything we have proceeds from His hand. The Lord is worthy to be lifted up and given the foremost position. Anything we have of riches, honor, majesty or abundance originates with God, and He holds dominion over it all. The Lord our God has the capability and the strength to accomplish whatever He intends. He watches over us and cares for us. He values us highly and raises us up. He gives us strength, confirms us in His way for us and brings us recovery and healing.

The greatness and glory of the Lord was very clear in David's mind. It is small wonder that God describes him as "a man after my own heart" (Acts 13:22). David seems to have come to understand more about the spirit of worship than any single individual in Scripture, barring, of course, the Lord Jesus Himself. The many psalms that David wrote were borne out of the attributes and character of the God we worship.

Magnify the Lord

Repeatedly in the Psalms, David implores us to "Glorify the LORD with me; let us exalt his name together" (Psalm 34:3). Have you ever thought about how to glorify the Lord? *Glorify* and *exalt* have also been translated as "magnify" or "make greater." But how do you magnify God, who fills the universe and beyond?

Think about two magnifying devices we use: a telescope and a microscope. We use a telescope to reach out into the heavens and gain perspective on things we cannot grasp. We use a microscope to draw in close to an object and see detail we would otherwise miss.

Likewise, when we magnify the Lord, we gain a better perspective by reaching out to Him, yet we also draw in close to Him and recognize the detail of His workings on our behalf. However it may be, we can't make God bigger than He is, but our understanding can become bigger than it is. And so the Scriptures help us magnify the Lord.

Five key attributes of God

Theologians have defined five central aspects of God's character. He has many wonderful traits, of course, but these five attributes are the essential characteristics unique to God. They tell us that the Lord is *eternal, almighty, omnipresent, all-knowing* and *holy.*

That God is *eternal* means that He embraces all time. God doesn't have to wait until next week to find out what's happening on the other side of it. He's there before us. The God we worship is sufficient for all our tomorrows. And though our finite minds cannot contain it, the fact is that God encompasses past, present and future. We worship a God who transcends time.

The Bible emphasizes this repeatedly: Abraham "called upon the name of the LORD, the Eternal God" (Genesis 21:33), Isaiah said "Trust in the LORD forever, for the LORD, the LORD, is the Rock eternal" (Isaiah 26:4), and Paul prayed "Now to the King eternal, immortal, invisible, the only God, be honor and glory for ever and ever. Amen" (1 Timothy 1:17).

God is *almighty.* The Lord revealed Himself in this way to both Abraham and Jacob: "I am God Almighty" (Genesis 17:1; 35:11), and the prophets called Him this. Obviously, this means that there are no restrictions to His power. The Lord created and sustains the entire universe by the word of His power, and He who brought all worlds into being is sufficiently capable to handle anything you and I face.

God is *omnipresent.* That simply means that He is everywhere. David wrote of God, "Where can I go from your Spirit? Where can I flee from your presence? If I go up to the heavens, you are there; if I make my bed in the depths, you are there. If I rise on the wings of the dawn, if I settle on the far side of the sea, even there your hand will guide me, your right hand will hold me fast" (Psalm 139:7–10). The Lord is with His people always and everywhere, and He will never leave nor forsake us. He is a God who has come alongside us. Praise His name.

God is *all-knowing.* *Omniscient* is the classic philosophical word for this. God, who is in the past, the present and the future, also knows every detail about the past, the present and the future. David went on, "If I say, 'Surely the darkness will hide me and the light become night around me,' even the darkness will not be dark to you; the night will shine like the day, for darkness is as light to you" (Psalm 139:11–12). There is nothing He does not know. Yet though He is fully aware of all our sins and weaknesses, He is gracious. He forgives our sins and is able to strengthen us in all our weakness.

Finally, the God we worship is *holy*. This means that He will never be less than He is; He will never act out of character. Holiness is the trait of God that tells us that God is complete in and of Himself. He wants to work that same holiness in our lives and bring us to a state of completeness and wholeness.

So God is eternal, almighty, omnipresent, all-knowing and holy, and these five attributes are unique to God. There is no other like Him.

Study questions:

1. Name some of the attributes of God that David expressed.
2. What does it mean to "glorify" or "magnify" the Lord, and how do we do it?
3. What are the five unique attributes of God?
4. What do these have to do with His worthiness to be worshiped?
5. Is this the God you worship?

4

The Beauty of Worship

Out of the context of God's holiness, the Lord provides a special glory to those who worship Him. As the Scripture says, "Worship the LORD in the splendor of his holiness" (1 Chronicles 16:29). In the King James Version, this is translated "the beauty of holiness."

I used to wonder how this could be. How could we ever be beautiful enough to worship God? But the Bible is speaking of a splendor, or beauty, that flows out of worship. Worship is intended to cultivate a wholeness and order in us that becomes a source of beauty in our lives. Remember, God really doesn't need our worship. We need to worship Him!

In this chapter we will study how holiness and beauty are related, based on Isaiah's vision of the Lord. We will begin to understand how God's holiness works in us to produce beauty.

Holiness and beauty

In the Book of Isaiah, there is a very significant insight that centers on this concept of beauty, or splendor. It also has to do with the wholeness that comes as we worship God's holiness.

This is the well-known passage in Isaiah 6 where the young Isaiah is worshiping in the temple. Suddenly he has a vision: "I saw the Lord seated on a throne, high and exalted, and the train of his robe filled the temple" (verse 1). The tangible presence of the glory of the Lord filled the house, and the place was shaken. Isaiah then goes on to describe his vision of angelic beings worshiping the Lord, crying out, "Holy, holy, holy is the LORD Almighty; the whole earth is full of his glory" (verse 3).

The issue of God's holiness is at the heart of this matter of splendor. God's holiness means He is complete and cannot lose this completeness. It is closely related to the similar-sounding word *wholeness*. The same traits that contribute to the beauty of an object are also wrapped up in the idea of holiness: completeness, perfection, order, unity and integrity.

Perhaps it is easy to see that completeness and perfection are inherent within the definition of *holiness*. But it may be less obvious how order and unity fit into the definition. Yet if we consider any kind of structure, it is clear that there must be order and unity if the structure is to remain whole.

Consider the building that you live in. It obviously did not come about as the result of lumber and concrete being thrown around in a random way. The various parts must be in proper relationship to each other, and there must be order. Furthermore, different parts must contribute to a common end; for instance, the walls help to support the roof. A well-designed building has a unified purpose. The order and unity of the structure are necessary for its wholeness.

These same traits contribute to something's beauty. Completeness is necessary so that a work of art can be seen in its full glory. Often an incomplete project looks like a terrible mess! Imagine a famous painting, such as *The Last Supper,* with all of its blue pigments lost. This incompleteness would subtract from its beauty.

Consider again *The Last Supper,* imagining that it was cut into several hundred square patches that were then scattered or rearranged at random. The order and unity of the painting would be destroyed, and the beauty would be lost. Consequently, we see that these characteristics are common to beauty and to holiness.

Holiness and provision

Let's return to Isaiah's vision of the throne of God. When he saw the Lord, he was struck by His awesome holiness and said "Woe to me!" (Isaiah 6:5). The Hebrew word there is *oy-li,* similiar to the colloquial Yiddish exclamation *oy vay.* By coming face to face with the holiness of God, Isaiah was made profoundly aware of his own incompleteness and shortcoming. He said, "I am ruined! For I am a man of unclean lips, and I live among a people of unclean lips, and my eyes have seen the King, the LORD Almighty" (verse 5).

Isaiah records that one of the angelic creatures flew to him with a live coal from the altar of God. The seraph touched Isaiah's mouth and said, "See, this has touched your lips; your guilt is taken away and your sin atoned for" (verse 7).

So there was cleansing, and there was then a call. The Lord said, "Whom shall I send? And who will go for us?" (verse 8). In the renewed strength that came from his worship experience, Isaiah said, "Here am I! Send me!" (verse 8).

This is the glory of worship. Even though we are incomplete, unworthy and inadequate, we are able to come into the presence of the most holy God. And as we worship Him, He will come and touch us with His life and power. By His touch He will purge us and prepare us for the next stage of our life and service to Him.

God's holiness is not revealed to intimidate us. He doesn't say, "Look how holy I am! Now I will humiliate you." He says, "Come into the presence of My holiness, and there you will discover your need. But fear not: My holiness is designed to answer your need."

Through Jesus Christ the wholeness of God's holiness is transmitted to us, to make us whole. He provides the complete answer to our human insufficiency. The angel put the coal of fire on Isaiah's lips, but I am persuaded that if Isaiah had said that his heart, his mind, his hands or his feet needed cleaning, that's exactly where the response to his worship would have brought the searing cleansing of God's fire.

In the beauty of worship, we come and see His awesome holiness. It comes not to destroy us, but to burn out the things that are unclean or unworthy. And in the process we become empowered to serve and to follow the Lord. Let's learn the beauty of worship as we come into His presence.

Study questions:

1. How are beauty and holiness related?
2. What does holiness have to do with wholeness and integrity?

3. What does Isaiah's vision tell us about the experience of worship?
4. How does God deal with our uncleanness and our inadequacy?
5. Is this the way you experience worship?

5

The Feast of Worship

This is my body

"This is my body that is broken for you."
This is the covenant that Christ now renews;
"My life for yours, that your life may be mine.
This bread is my body, my blood is this wine."

Eat now and drink, taking life into your soul;
And feast on the promise, let Jesus make you whole.
Health for your weakness and forgiveness anew;
Take now, "This is my body that is broken for you."

Jack W. Hayford,
copyright 1981 by Pilot Point Music,
a division of Nazarene Publishing House

In this chapter we will study the terms used for the Lord's Table, and the significance of the elements. We will also look at the barriers to coming to the Lord's Table, so that they can be understood and overcome.

Titles for the Lord's Table

There is nothing more central to the worship life of the Church than that which Jesus founded by His death and resurrection—the feast of worship at the Lord's Table. It's called many different things. In some places it's called the Mass. Others call it the Eucharist. For others it's Communion or the breaking of bread. For still others, it's the Lord's Table. Each one of these terms is significant, so let's discuss each briefly.

The *Mass* focuses on the presence of the Lord. Jesus said that whenever we gather in His name, He is in the midst of us. When we come together at the Lord's Table, it is most appropriate to recognize that He is with us. In Exodus 33:15–16, Moses said to the Lord, "If your Presence does not go with us, do not send us up from here. How will anyone know that you are pleased with me and with your people unless you go with us? What else will distinguish me and your people from all the other people on the face of the earth?"

Moses made it clear that he never wanted to be away from the presence of the Lord. At the Lord's Table we should have the same focus: "Lord, let Your Presence be with us now and with us always."

The term *Eucharist* is derived from the Greek word *eucharistao*, which means "thanksgiving." That term focuses on coming to the Lord's Table with thanksgiving for the work that Jesus did and the provision He made for us through His death and resurrection.

In my childhood experience, the time of coming to the Lord's Table was somber to the point of depression. Everyone was very grave and serious, and of course there should be an appropriate reverence for the Lord's Table. But the Lord also wants us to remember His victory!

It was through Jesus' death and resurrection that all the powers of hell were overcome, and the Bible tells us that Jesus made a public spectacle of the powers of hell and triumphed over them (Colossians 2:15). So we come to the Lord's Table with praise and thanksgiving for the victory and provision through Jesus' suffering on the cross.

When we speak of *Communion,* the focus is on our fellowship together. We come together in united participation to meet with Him, and we also come in fellowship with one another. This fellowship has two purposes: to share our testimonies of victory and to share our trials and be strengthened.

Revelation 12:11 tells us that there is a power in our testimony that overcomes the works of the devil; so when we come together to the Lord's Table, it is a natural time to attest to what the Lord has done. We can also share our trials or weakness and allow the provision of the Lord's Table and the strength of brothers and sisters to bring edification and encouragement. None of us are so strong that we don't need each other. "As iron sharpens iron," Proverbs 27:17 tells us, "so one man sharpens another."

Breaking bread refers to Jesus' symbolic distribution of the bread at the table. In Luke 22:19, we read that Jesus "took bread, gave thanks and broke it, and gave it to them, saying, 'This is my body given for you.'" The breaking of the bread represented the breaking of His own body that was to take place as Jesus took all of our sin upon Himself and dealt with it on the cross.

We use the word *broken* for relationships that have been damaged—"They broke up." We use it for bodies that are sick and disabled—"His health was broken." We may even use it when we are in trouble economically—"I'm broke." Each time we come to receive of the Lord's Table, Jesus is saying, "Remember, I have made provision for where you have been broken, that you might have completeness. I was broken so that you don't have to be."

When we speak of *the Lord's Table,* we're noting the fact that He is the one who serves the table. He comes there as host. Though human hands attend to its preparation and distribute the elements as we participate, Jesus is the Lord at the table to which He has called us all to come.

In Luke 22:15, Jesus says, "I have eagerly desired to eat this Passover with you before I suffer." He has already sent Peter and John to go and make preparations for this meal. Then in verse 19 He says, "Do this in remembrance of me." Thus we have a direct commandment that we too are to come to the table and are not to neglect this practice.

The truth of the Lord's Table

When we come to the Lord's Table, we need to be sure we understand its meaning.

We take the bread, which Jesus said was "my body, which is [broken] for you" (1 Corinthians 11:24). He is specifically reminding us of what He has accomplished for us. Even His coming to the earth and taking flesh was for our benefit. So partake of the bread, remembering what He says.

Jesus also made clear the meaning of the cup when He gave

thanks and offered it to the disciples: "Drink from i you. This is my blood of the covenant, which is poure~~d out for~~ many for the forgiveness of sins" (Matthew 26:27–28). There is nothing we need more than forgiveness! Although our salvation was assured when we came to Christ as Savior, we need regular cleansing from the things that daily soil our lives. Come and partake of the cup, realizing that forgiveness is ours.

The triumph of the Lord's Table

There are two primary barriers to participation in the feast of the Lord's Table: neglect and fear. People neglect this celebration because they're unaware that it's something that Jesus commanded, and they don't understand the magnitude of the provision released through this practice. Jesus commands us to "Do this" because He wants us to find victory in His own triumph. Don't neglect this. Come to the Lord's Table, whether in the privacy of your own home or in public worship.

But there is another barrier: fear. People say, "I feel so unworthy. And isn't there a verse in the Bible that says that if you partake unworthily you might die?" The verse people are thinking of is in 1 Corinthians 11:26–30:

> For whenever you eat this bread and drink this cup, you proclaim the Lord's death until he comes.
> Therefore, whoever eats the bread or drinks the cup of the Lord in an unworthy manner will be guilty of sinning against the body and blood of the Lord. A man ought to examine himself before he eats of the bread and drinks of the cup. For anyone who eats and drinks without recognizing the body of the Lord eats and drinks judgment on himself. That is why many among you are weak and sick, and a number of you have fallen asleep.

This is one of the most misunderstood passages in the Word of God. In saying that we need to partake "worthily," Paul wants us to understand the full value in what we are doing. We need to allow the power that Jesus has provided in this practice to come to bear on our situation.

Through the practice of Communion, the Lord has provided healing and restoration for our brokenness. But if we don't recognize that, then we can't let that power come and affect our situation. So Paul is actually saying, "Some of you are sick and some have even died because you aren't recognizing that there is healing power in this practice."

The Bible is not saying that if you partake unworthily you'll die because you need forgiveness and wholeness. Rather, it says that if you don't take of the abundance of what is provided, you will miss the opportunity for healing. We're encouraged to come and receive, knowing that there is power, goodness, and healing available in the Lord's Table for every need.

Jesus died and rose from the dead for us. Receive the abundance of the provision that is available through them for whatever circumstances you face. They will nourish you and make you strong for tomorrow. That's the feast of worship.

Study questions:

1. What do you call the Lord's Table? What does that mean to you?
2. Has reading about the significance of other names for the Lord's Table enriched your understanding of this scriptural practice? In what way?
3. Why does the Lord command us to come, eat and drink at His table?
4. Have neglect or fear been barriers for you?
5. If so, what are you missing? And what are you waiting for?

6

The Fullness of Worship

It's a warm summer morning, and in a small church forty or fifty people sit listening to the soporific drone of the sermon. A few aisles from the front, an old man snores despite his wife's occasional nudges. Near the back, a young woman carefully files her nails. Throughout the room people are in various stages of preoccupation as the preacher monotonously drones on. This is how some people view a "worship service."

Many people have experienced "worship" as dull and monotonous. I sympathize. I've seen more of that in church services than most people, because I've had more years to see it. But I've also seen a lot of fullness in worship. We can see this in the birth of the Church and in the apostle Paul's instruction.

Jesus spoke of a kind of worship that has nothing to do with weekly drudgery: "Yet a time is coming and has now come when the true worshipers will worship the Father in spirit and truth, for they are the kind of worshipers the Father seeks. God is spirit, and his worshipers must worship in spirit and in truth" (John 4:23–24).

In this chapter we will study the Lord's directive for worship and see how it was exemplified in the early Church. We will also look at what Paul said about worship.

The Savior's directive

I want to talk about the fullness of worship. Jesus gave a clear instruction that will make worship anything but dull and monotonous if we're willing to obey it. He said that we must worship God "in spirit and in truth." That's His remedy for dullness and monotony!

31

Jesus was saying that God doesn't like the dullness that comes when people make verbal sounds of worship but don't allow the work of the Spirit into their lives. Worshiping in spirit and in truth means letting the Holy Spirit bring life to your worship, and worshiping according to the truth of the revelation of God. Let's look at each of these points more closely.

Worshiping in spirit can only happen when we are alive and glowing with the Spirit. We're alive because we've been born again; we're aglow because we've been baptized in the Holy Spirit. When we let the Holy Spirit bring life and energy to our worship, it turns it into something of fresh, life-changing vibrancy.

Worshiping in truth means that we are worshiping God as He really is, not as we would like Him to be. In earlier chapters we talked about the God we worship and why it is important to worship Him as He is and according to His way. Maintaining the truth in worship is a key to maintaining its life.

The risen Jesus breathed on His disciples and said, "Receive the Holy Spirit" (John 20:22). Our worship can become a vibrant connecting time between us and the Father, with whom we've been born into relationship. He calls us to a dynamic worship experience each time we come before Him.

The Church's beginning

This fullness of worship was manifest at the Church's birth. We see the Holy Spirit coming with power, and the proclamation of the Word with power. What Jesus directed became the Church's experience at its inception.

The Bible records that on the day the Church was born, everyone was filled with the Holy Spirit and worshiped God. They were recognizably worshiping even though they were supernaturally speaking with many different languages— speaking in tongues. The Bible says that visitors from many nations were drawn to the sound of the disciples' praise and understood their different languages: "We hear them declaring the wonders of God in our own tongues!" (Acts 2:11). This amazing phenomenon brought inquiry that was answered by the teaching of the Word. Peter got up and declared the Gospel with power, and the results were dramatic.

So the Church was born in a worship service, and we see that the incorporation of Spirit-filled worship and the truth of the Word characterized the Church from its very beginning. Both our native language and spiritual languages are to be used in our worship. Continually being filled with the Spirit keeps the fullness of worship.

The apostle's instruction

In 1 Corinthians 14, Paul corrects some of the excesses and abuses in the people's use of spiritual gifts: "Follow the way of love and eagerly desire spiritual gifts, especially the gift of prophecy. For anyone who speaks in a tongue does not speak to men but to God. Indeed, no one understands him; he utters mysteries with his spirit. But everyone who prophesies speaks to men for their strengthening, encouragement and comfort. He who speaks in a tongue edifies himself, but he who prophesies edifies the church" (1 Corinthians 14:1–4). Paul is concerned that when they are using the gift of tongues in a public meeting without interpretation, it will be confusing to inquirers and will not build up those who don't understand: "You may be giving thanks well enough, but the other man is not edified" (verse 17). However, we must not ignore the positive side of his comments about their enthusiastic worship. He is saying that we are doing a good job worshiping when we use the added capacity that the spiritual language gives us.

In the privacy of my room, I may at any time lift up my voice to my Father, worshiping in the Spirit. Even though the language is not known to me, the fullness and warmth of worship overflows as I exalt Him who is worthy. By that means, I give thanks well and am keeping my heart filled with His Spirit.

When I'm gathered with the brothers and sisters in a public assembly, the use of the spiritual language may not always be appropriate. But the fire of the Spirit is still present, keeping everything aflame with His power and presence. The use of prophecy, which convicts sinners and lays bare the secrets of hearts, can convict inquirers and unbelievers, leading them to worship themselves; "So he will fall down and worship God, exclaiming, 'God is really among you!'" (1 Corinthians 14:25).

Furthermore, the apostle tells us in verse 26 that the truth of the Word is vital in our worship services as well: "What then shall we say, brothers? When you come together, everyone has a hymn, or a word of instruction, a revelation, a tongue or an interpretation. All of these must be done for the strengthening of the church."

There is a saying that if we just have the Word, we'll dry up, and if we just have the Spirit, we'll blow up! But if we have the Word of truth and the Spirit together, we'll grow up. The fullness of worship is realized when people act according to the rule of love and find the appropriate place for both the Spirit and the Word.

We should live in the continued blessing of the Church's beginning, understanding that Spirit-filled worship is what God always intended. Let's do as Jesus said and worship in spirit and in truth.

Study questions:

1. What is your usual experience of worship? Is it full of life or boring and monotonous?
2. What did the Lord mean by His command to "worship in spirit and in truth"?
3. Describe the central place of worship in the Church's birth.
4. How can we find a balance in the use of spiritual gifts in public worship?
5. Do you tend to neglect either the Word or the Spirit?

7

The Song of Worship

In a stone-built church a congregation begins its meeting by singing songs that are hundreds of years old. Elsewhere a small group meets in a home and sings a chorus of praise that one of them wrote the day before. In a great European cathedral a full orchestra and choir praise God with song, while in an Indian village a man plays sitar for a handful of singers. Around the world, believers gather together with song.

And so it has been throughout history. We can follow church music back through the great hymns of the past few centuries, to the baroque oratorios of Bach and Handel, to the modal music and Gregorian chants of the medieval church. In fact, this singing tradition goes back to the first century: Scholars believe that some portions of Scripture were hymns of the early Church.

Christianity has been called the singing faith. It is a verifiable fact that none of the world's religions have the kind of song found among those who are alive in Christ. There's something about the life of the Spirit that begets a song, and singing is probably the most widespread worship form throughout the Church.

In this chapter we will study the command to sing and the power of singing. It will help us to see why we are directed to worship with song, and give examples of the release of God's power through song.

The command to sing

The Bible repeatedly and directly tells us that singing releases joy. It's easy to sing when the joy of the Lord fills our hearts.

But we are told to do it at other times as well! When we study the Psalms, we see David singing to the Lord in the middle of some difficult situations. It's not always, "He put a new song in my mouth, a hymn of praise to our God" (Psalm 40:3). Sometimes it is, "In my anguish I cried to the LORD" (Psalm 118:5). In other psalms he confesses sin or expresses sorrow.

It is clear that we don't just sing when we feel happy or excited. We do it because the Word commands it and because power is released through singing. Even when we don't feel like it, and even when it may not be very appealing at a particular juncture in our lives, it's good to lift our voices to praise and worship Him.

Let's look at how firmly the tradition of singing is rooted in the Scriptures. There are 85 places in the Bible where we are directed to sing. Psalm 47 alone commands us to sing five times!

> Clap your hands, all you nations;
>   shout to God with cries of joy....
> Sing praises to God, sing praises;
>   sing praises to our King, sing praises.
> For God is the King of all the earth;
>   sing to him a psalm of praise.
>
> Psalm 47:1, 6–7

Psalm 150 invites us to use all the instruments and says, Let everything that has breath praise the LORD. Praise the LORD.

Not all the directives to sing are in the Book of Psalms. Paul tells the Colossians, "Be thankful. Let the word of Christ dwell in you richly as you teach and admonish one another with all wisdom, and as you sing psalms, hymns and spiritual songs with gratitude in your hearts to God" (Colossians 3:15–16).

We are directed to let singing spring out of our joy. James instructs: "Is anyone happy? Let him sing songs of praise" (James 5:13). Psalm 98:1 says, "Sing to the LORD a new song, for he has done marvelous things; his right hand and his holy arm have worked salvation for him." That kind of song is born out of God's recent victories in our lives.

Psalm 98 is also just one of eight places in the Scriptures where we're instructed to "sing a new song." This is not a command that can only be fulfilled by a very creative person or gifted musician. Rather, it directs us to allow the vibrancy of the new things Jesus is doing in us *now* to find expression.

At times of triumph and rejoicing, come and sing to the Lord. If your prayer now is one of mourning, then sing it to him worshipfully. You can sing, "Lord, I give you my pain, but I bring it with a song because you are the one who gives songs in the night" (see Job 35:10). Sing a new song.

Finally, Ephesians 5:18–20 says, "Be filled with the Spirit. Speak to one another with psalms, hymns and spiritual songs. Sing and make music in your heart to the Lord, always giving thanks to God the Father for everything." This indicates that singing in the Spirit is a way to keep filled with the Spirit. Singing releases joy, it refreshes and renews us even in times of pain, and it helps us maintain a fresh flow of the Spirit of the Lord in and through our lives.

The power of singing

The Bible tells us that singing brings forth life, overcomes obstacles, releases victory and is creative in its impact.

In Isaiah 54:1, song is linked with the birthing of new life.

> "Sing, O barren woman,
>   you who never bore a child;
> burst into song, shout for joy,
>   you who were never in labor;
> because more are the children of the desolate woman
>   than of her who has a husband,
>   says the LORD.

What do you want to see brought forth in your life? Sing about it to the Lord. Let the creativity of His vital power surge through you, and His Spirit fill you to overflowing.

Singing breaks down walls and opens doors. Paul and Silas were chained in a prison cell in Philippi, but when they sang praises, the Lord brought release. That night, even as they sang, there was an earthquake, the doors of the prison opened and their chains fell off.

People who sing in the midst of bondage can find that deliverance comes through the power of a song. Psalm 32:7 says, "You are my hiding place; You will protect me from trouble and surround me with songs of deliverance." God hides us and preserves us from trouble by encircling us with songs of deliverance!

Singing is a way to gain victory, even when we face tremendous opposition. Second Chronicles 20 tells us how King Jehoshaphat and the nation of Israel, though greatly outnumbered by their enemy, went out to battle with the choir leading them. Their song of victory brought confusion to their adversaries, so the enemy was confounded and actually turned on each other.

Likewise, the Lord calls us to worship Him with song when faced with an enemy that is too strong for us. Our song can be filled with power and life. We will find victory in our circumstances as we obey the directive to worship with song.

Song is creative. In Job 38:4–7 we are told that the original work of God's creation was accompanied by the singing of the angelic hosts. "The morning stars sang together and all the angels shouted for joy" (verse 7)!

What is there in your life that is yet to be created? What needs to be brought into being where now you see nothing? Sing! And see the creative power of God burst forth to that accompaniment.

There is power in singing, as in all worship, and wherever we welcome the King through our offerings of obedient worship, the Kingdom begins to happen.

Study questions:

1. What is unique about the Christian faith in terms of singing?
2. How often does the Bible command us to sing, and in what circumstances?
3. How does singing bring victory and overcome obstacles? Give some biblical examples.
4. What does singing have to do with the creation of new life?
5. Have you experienced the power of singing in your own life?

8

The Language of Worship

We have looked at several aspects of worship. There are distinct aspects to human nature, and worship gives expression to each.

In the next three chapters, we will be discussing how different parts of our being are used in expressing worship to the Lord. We will see how the intellect, the emotions, and the body are all called into participation in the act of worship. But first, let's look at how God designed us for worship.

In this chapter we will see how God made us as three-part beings and intended us for worship. We will study six different aspects of worship in prayer and discern what quality makes them worship.

The structure of human beings

God has made us as three-part beings: spirit, soul and body. Our spirit is the part of our being that God made especially for relating to Him. Only God can satisfy that part of our being, and apart from Him our spirit has no life. Our spirit is our God-consciousness.

Our soul is what we are. Genesis 2:7 describes the creation of Adam like this: "The Lord God formed the man from the dust of the ground and breathed into his nostrils the breath of life, and the man became a living being." Each person could be described as a soul within a body, either spiritually alive or spiritually dead. The soul is essentially our intellect (thoughts), our emotions (feelings) and our will (choices). We could call the soul our *self-consciousness*.

Our body really needs no explanation! But it is our window

to the natural world. With our bodies we interface with the physical dimension. We could call the body our *world-consciousness*.

So we are spiritual beings, intellectual beings, emotional beings and physical beings.

Six aspects of prayer

As intellectual creatures, we have the power of speech. That's what sets us apart from the rest of the species on this planet. It's what makes us, under God, lords of the earth—the ones He has placed in charge.

Speech is what gives us the capacity to function effectively in discharging the responsibilities God has given us to govern in life. These responsibilities may include our families, our businesses and our relationships. The Lord enables us to sensibly and sensitively think through these issues as we talk to Him in prayer. The language of worship is found in such prayer.

In Psalm 65:2, David writes: "O you who hear prayer, to you all men will come." Our prayer is offered in several ways, all of which can be filled with worship when they are brought into submission to Him. The Lord's Prayer concludes, "for Yours is the kingdom and the power and the glory forever. Amen" (Matthew 6:13, NKJV). That's the worship summary statement of our prayer: Everything is His.

Let's look at the different aspects of prayer.

The first is *confession*. Even though gross sin may not be a part of our lives, we must come to God each day with contrite hearts for refinement and cleansing. In biblical times, people practiced foot washing for the very practical reason that their feet became dirty just from walking along the dusty roads. Likewise, we must be cleansed regularly, if for no other reason than that we have been exposed to the dirty conditions that characterize the world.

We also need to recognize that even when we do well, we still do not measure up to God's standard. Sin is missing the mark of that high standard. We don't need to condemn ourselves; we simply need to come before God and say, "Lord,

I'm growing in Your ways, but I'm not there yet. Forgive my shortcomings and continue to shape me into Your image."

If we do fall into gross disobedience or failure, we need to come quickly for forgiveness with repentant hearts. The Bible tells us that we have an Advocate who will plead our case before God and who has paid the penalty for all our sin.

Secondly, we have been given the privilege of *petition*. John 15:7 records Jesus saying, "If you remain in me and my words remain in you, ask whatever you wish, and it will be given you." We all face needs. Jesus directed us to pray for the provision of our daily bread. There are situations where we need help, strength, healing or wisdom. But in our petition we may also ask, "Lord, what do You want me to do? How should I direct the details of my life? I submit them to You and in all my ways acknowledge You, that You may direct my paths." We come and ask for His grace to meet our needs and His guidance to make decisions.

Thirdly, we come to *praise* him. We "enter his gates with thanksgiving and his courts with praise" (Psalm 100:4). There is a distinction between praise and thanksgiving. Praise expresses worship for who God is—His character and His attributes. Thanksgiving, on the other hand, is worshiping the Lord for what He has done. One missionary had to work out the meaning of these terms with his native helper when they were translating the Bible. They determined that thanksgiving is saying, "Lord, *it* is good," while praise is saying, "Lord, *You* are good."

When we praise God, we are remembering His goodness for every day that is behind us and before us. Then, stepping into His presence, we wait there to receive His guidance and direction.

Fourthly, we are directed to *meditate*. "O God, we meditate on your unfailing love" (Psalm 48:9). For the believer, this is not a transcendental, New-Age trip! Christian meditation has an object: We meditate on the Lord and His Word. Psalm 119 speaks seven times of meditating on the precepts, decrees, wonders, statutes and promises of God. We think over and mentally digest what He is saying to us. We linger in God's presence, waiting for His voice to us.

Fifthly, *intercession and supplication* are great privileges of believers. Whatever the trouble is, in ourselves or in the world around us, we can invoke the power of God, contracting with the Almighty for His strength. Through spiritual warfare, we can address any situation where people are suffering from the press of circumstances or the attack of the enemy.

Intercession is the responsibility of every believer. Scripture directs us to pray for our governmental leaders and all who are in authority, for both practical and spiritual reasons. Paul wrote to Timothy, "I urge, then, first of all, that requests, prayers, intercession and thanksgiving be made for everyone—for kings and all those in authority, that we may live peaceful and quiet lives in all godliness and holiness. This is good, and pleases God our Savior, who wants all people to be saved and to come to a knowledge of the truth" (1 Timothy 2:1–4). We step into the gap, asking for the goodness and mercy of God to work in every circumstance.

Sixthly, we are commanded to *exalt and adore* Him who is worthy. "Exalt the LORD our God and worship at his footstool; he is holy" (Psalm 99:5). From the most ancient writings of Scripture to the eternal future, we see the Lord God being exalted. He is worthy because He is the Creator and Sustainer of all things. He is worthy because He has redeemed us from darkness.

The language of worship is found in prayer. In these various ways, human beings glorify the living God and come before His throne for everything they need.

Study questions:

1. What does the way we're created have to do with our capacity to worship?
2. What are the six types of prayer mentioned?
3. How can you explain the difference between thanksgiving and praise?
4. In what way are intercession and supplication great privileges and also responsibilities?
5. Are you making use of all the languages of worship in prayer?

9

The Humility in Worship

In the last chapter we saw that human beings are made up of spirit, soul and body, with the capacity to reason and communicate in the language of worship. Now we will look at our emotions and their appropriate function in worship.

I am not talking about wild emotionalism. Some people are so "red hot" about their worship that they seem fanatical. On the other hand, some people are ice cold in their worship. We want to keep the good of our intellect, while being full-hearted, with warmth, vibrancy and vitality in our worship.

God looks on the heart, not on the outward appearance.

> For this is what the high and lofty One says—
> he who lives for ever, whose name is holy:
> "I live in a high and holy place,
>   but also with him who is contrite and lowly in spirit,
> to revive the spirit of the lowly
>   and to revive the heart of the contrite."
>
> Isaiah 57:15

In this chapter we will look at the story of the return of the Ark of the Covenant to Jerusalem. We will come to know the qualities of David that made him a man after God's own heart. We will discover the importance of worshiping God's way and see both the power of humility and the disastrous consequences of pride.

The heart of David

David is the classic case study of a person who worships. He was a worshiper par excellence, and he knew the importance of humility in worship.

In Psalm 51, which David wrote after falling into sin, he came to the Lord with confession and repentance. He said:

> Have mercy on me, O God,
>   according to your unfailing love;
> according to your great compassion
>   blot out my transgressions.
> Wash away all my iniquity
>   and cleanse me from my sin.
> For I know my transgressions,
>   and my sin is always before me....
> Create in me a pure heart, O God,
>   and renew a steadfast spirit within me.
> Do not cast me from your presence
>   or take your Holy Spirit from me.
> Restore to me the joy of your salvation
>   and grant me a willing spirit, to sustain me....
> The sacrifices of God are a broken spirit;
> A broken and contrite heart,
>   O God, you will not despise.
>
> Psalm 51:1–3, 10–12, 17

It was not only in confession that David humbled himself. In Psalm 131 David said:

> My heart is not proud, O LORD,
>   my eyes are not haughty;
> I do not concern myself with great matters
>   or things too wonderful for me.
> But I have stilled and quieted my soul;
>   like a weaned child with its mother,
>   like a weaned child is my soul within me.
>
> Verses 1–2

We will also look at a story of how David manifested this humility in worship.

The humanness of David

The passion that David had for worship is shown in a heart that desired the presence of God. Here we will study the account of David's longing to bring the Ark of the Covenant into the city of Jerusalem.

The Ark was the center of the presence of God in ancient Israel. The glory of the Lord dwelled over the Ark, and David knew that this presence was something to be desired greatly. He had a passion for it, and he pursued it with diligence. Yet his first attempts to move the Ark ended in tragedy.

It is in 2 Samuel 6 that we read of how David desired to bring the Ark up to Jerusalem. He gathered the people together, and they built a new cart in which to take the Ark of the Covenant to the place that David had prepared. Two men, Ahio and Uzzah, drove the cart while the people praised. Notice that they had a good plan to accomplish the work of the Lord, and they were even praising God. But carrying out a program in a human way is almost invariably not God's way.

If David had looked into the Scripture to discover God's way, he would have found that the Ark was always to be carried on poles. It was never to be carried in a cart, and it was never to be touched.

As the people were going up to Jerusalem, the oxen pulling the cart stumbled. Uzzah reached out to steady the Ark. The judgment of the Lord came against Uzzah for that act of disobedience and irreverence, and he was struck dead.

David's response to that judgment was anger and fear. He was angry because he was trying to do a great thing, yet God responded in judgment. He was also afraid when he saw the mighty, sovereign hand of the Lord upholding His own law. David had received another glimpse of his own imperfection and lack of holiness.

But David's desire for God's presence wasn't wrong. He left the Ark at the house of Obed-Edom, near the place where Uzzah had been struck dead. The Lord blessed Obed-Edom and his entire household for the time that the Ark remained there. So David learned another lesson in humility: When you worship, you do it God's way.

The humility of David

Three months after this incident, David did bring the Ark to Jerusalem. He discovered that obedience and praise are the keys to welcoming God's presence into your midst.

David had learned the wisdom of following the Word and way of the Lord. He humbly turned from his original plan and followed God's instructions for carrying the Ark. And as they drew near the city, his rejoicing overflowed into a dance. In his humility, he laid aside his kingly garments and began to dance before the Lord. That spirit of praise and rejoicing was a delight to the Lord, but there was another person who saw it who was not so delighted.

David's wife, Michal, was infuriated. She thought that David was making a fool of himself and disgracing her. In 2 Samuel 6:20–23 we read:

> When David returned home to bless his household, Michal daughter of Saul came out to meet him and said, "How the king of Israel has distinguished himself today, disrobing in the sight of the slave girls of his servants as any vulgar fellow would!"
>
> David said to Michal, "It was before the LORD, who chose me rather than your father or anyone from his house when he appointed me ruler over the LORD's people Israel—I will celebrate before the LORD. I will become even more undignified than this, and I will be humiliated in my own eyes. But by these slave girls you spoke of, I will be held in honor."
>
> And Michal daughter of Saul had no children to the day of her death.

This is a message for all who are scornful of humble worship. Michal is like people who say, "I don't want too much emotion in church." Pure emotionalism without thought and discernment can be inappropriate. But without emotion we miss the bursting forth of praise and the joy that comes when people worship with all their hearts. Those who try to quench the spirit of worship are inviting God's displeasure.

Michal paid a heavy price for her cynicism and ridicule. David came with a blessing for his household, but Michal's pride instead brought a curse of barrenness upon her. Although Michal remained queen, she was not able to bring forth any new life. Meanwhile, David became a victorious king because humility characterized his worship.

Study questions:

1. Why is humility important in worship?
2. How do the Psalms reveal David's humble heart?
3. What do we learn from David's first attempt to bring the Ark of the Covenant back to Jerusalem?
4. What does the story in 2 Samuel 6:20–23 tell us about right attitudes toward worship?
5. Are you more like David or Michal in the way you worship?

10

The Sacrifices of Worship

We have already examined many facets of truth about worship. We have seen that to gain purpose and fulfillment in life, we must worship God on His terms. We have also looked at the way we are uniquely constructed as human beings. Intellectually, we need a language of worship, and we must also engage our emotions in worship with appropriate humility. Let's now deal with our bodies in worship.

Recently I was with a member of our congregation who represents a very well-known, worldwide corporation. He travels widely to help other businesspeople solve their problems. I watched him beginning a seminar with cool-headed, calculating executives by saying, "I'm asking for your response, and I want you to show me some skin." He meant that he wanted to actuate their responses by signaling with their hands and using active body language.

When we come to worship the Lord, I think He would say the same thing to us: "Show me some skin"! The Lord wants us to demonstrate our response actively, and He wants us to use our bodies to do so.

In this chapter we will study physical expressions of worship to the Lord. We will compare and contrast Old and New Testament worship and learn the meanings wrapped up in the Hebrew words for praise and worship.

The way of worship

The Bible is very explicit that we are to be actively involved in our worship. In Psalm 50:5 the Lord says, "Gather to me my consecrated ones, who made a covenant with me by sacrifice."

In the Old Testament, worshipers offered sacrifices of animals and grain, but that was not all that was required. The worshiper also came with praise and thanksgiving. Psalm 107:21–22 is one passage where we are explicitly told that thanksgiving is a sacrifice to the Lord:

> Let them give thanks to the Lord for his unfailing love
> and his wonderful deeds for men.
> Let them sacrifice thank offerings
> and tell of his works with songs of joy.

The New Testament also speaks of the need for sacrifice. Of course, the Old Testament system of sacrifice for atonement was fulfilled when Jesus Christ hung on the cross for us. He satisfied the justice of God with the sacrifice of Himself. It is through Him that we are granted the privilege of coming into God's presence in worship. But don't make any mistake—there are still sacrifices to be offered.

Five times the New Testament speaks of sacrifice, exclusive of the numerous references to the sacrifice of the Lord Jesus for our sin. These five passages all refer to actions or actual physical things.

In Philippians 2:17 Paul speaks of himself as a sacrifice: "But even if I am being poured out like a drink offering on the sacrifice and service coming from your faith, I am glad and rejoice with all of you." When Paul wrote to the Philippians, he was in prison and knew that he could be facing death. This is perhaps the most dramatic example of sacrifice. In the world today, many people face martyrdom for their faith, and this is precious in the Lord's sight—a literal sacrifice of their lives.

Nevertheless, all of us can make a sacrifice to God, as Paul said in Romans 12:1: "Therefore, I urge you, brothers, in view of God's mercy, to offer your bodies as living sacrifices, holy and pleasing to God—this is your spiritual act of worship." We are directed to no less than complete sacrifice of ourselves to the Lord. All other sacrifices are contained within that one.

Further on in Philippians, Paul speaks about a gift that the believers had sent to him, and he says that it was an acceptable sacrifice in the eyes of God. This verse echoes the sentiments of the writer of Hebrews, who tells us, "And do not forget to do good and to share with others, for with such sacrifices God is pleased" (Hebrews 13:16). Our giving and service, both to those who preach the Gospel and to those in need, is an important sacrifice to God, one that must never be neglected.

Remember that the basic meaning of *worship* is "to ascribe worth to." Therefore, presenting our bodies, our service and our praise is worship—acknowledging Him as God Most High.

The words of worship

In the Old Testament, particularly in the Psalms, we are repeatedly told to praise the Lord. However, each word used has different connotations about how we are to worship. Let's look at six Hebrew words and discover what they tell us about the physical aspect of worship.

The two words *yadah* and *todah* are closely related, and they account for many of the times the word *praise* appears in our Bibles. One example is in Psalm 54:6: "I will sacrifice a freewill offering to you; I will praise your name, O LORD, for it is good." In that verse the word *yadah* is translated "praise." But inherent in its meaning is the idea "to hold out the hands." The word *todah* also contains the sense of stretching out of the hands, but in this case it implies that it is to be done with a congregation or as part of a choir of worshipers. It is used in the title of Psalm 100: "A Psalm of praise" (KJV).

Another commonly used word for praise was *halal;* in fact, it is part of the word *hallelujah.* This word means to boast or to rave, indicating sincere and deep thanks. It is frequently used in the plural form in the Old Testament, indicating that the praise was to be expressed in the congregation. This is evident from 2 Chronicles 5:13: "The trumpeters and singers joined in unison, as with one voice, to give praise and thanks to the LORD."

There are three other words that we can study briefly. *Shabakh* is translated "praise" or "praised" a total of ten times. The primary idea behind this word is to praise with a loud voice. It can also be translated "glorify," as in Psalm 63:3: "Because your love is better than life, my lips will glorify you."

The word *zamar* is translated "praise" in Psalm 21:13, where it occurs in conjunction with singing: "Be exalted, O LORD, in your strength; we will sing and praise your might." This makes sense because *zamar* means "to praise with a musical instrument or with singing."

Finally, *barak* is translated "praise" on a few occasions. It contains the idea of bowing or kneeling in homage to God, and also of blessing or declaring someone blessed. That is how it is translated in Psalm 72:15: "May people ever pray for him and bless him all day long."

The work of worship

We have now seen that our sacrifice of worship is to involve our bodies and that physical action is implied in Hebrew words for praise. But throughout Scripture there is another reference to using our bodies to worship God. It begins with the sacrifice of our lips: "Through Jesus, therefore, let us continually offer to God a sacrifice of praise—the fruit of lips that confess his name" (Hebrews 13:15). The fruit of our lips is perhaps the most obvious aspect of sacrifice to include in a book on worship. The Bible tells us to sing, speak and even shout at times. This is not fanatical, mindless babbling, but a meaningful expression of worship and praise spoken aloud. In the Book of Psalms alone we are directed to speak or shout more than fifty times, and that doesn't include the numerous commands to sing. The Lord wants us to communicate to Him and to use our voices in His honor.

The Scripture shows us many ways to praise with our bodies. We kneel before His presence, showing our humility in our physical actions. Psalm 95:6 says, "Come, let us bow down in worship, let us kneel before the LORD our Maker." In Genesis 24:26 we also read of Abraham's servant bowing down in worship to the Lord. Philippians 2:10 tells us that every knee will bow to the Lord Jesus, in heaven and on earth and under the earth.

Hands are also often used in praise. We saw that two of the most common Hebrew words for praise indicated that the hands be stretched out. In Psalm 63:4 David writes, "I will praise you as long as I live, and in your name I will lift up my hands." Paul said, "I want men everywhere to lift up holy hands in prayer" (1 Timothy 2:8). Hands are also clapped in a declaration of His triumph. "Clap your hands, all you nations; shout to God with cries of joy," the psalmist says (Psalm 47:1).

Our heads may be raised up in a sense of releasing joy from the condemnation of the past: "Then my head will be exalted above the enemies who surround me; at his tabernacle will I sacrifice with shouts of joy" (Psalm 27:6). David says of the Lord in Psalm 3:3: "You bestow glory on me and lift up my head." We lift up our souls to the Lord (Psalm 143:8) and also our eyes, seeking His mercy (Psalm 123:1–2).

Although it is important that we have an intellectual language of worship, and that we are emotionally involved in our praise, we mustn't exclude the physical aspects of worship. Physical expressions of praise can help to keep us honest, open and committed. They engage us more fully in the act of worship. Worship with your body; it is a sacrifice pleasing to God.

Study questions:

1. Since Jesus has made a sacrifice for all time, how are we still called to make sacrifices to God?
2. In what way are sacrifices connected to physical actions?
3. What do the Hebrew words for praise tell us about using physical actions?
4. What does the Bible say about using our bodies in worship?
5. How obedient are you to the command to worship God using your body?

11

The Offerings of Worship

"I felt that the Lord wanted me to give a certain amount for our church's missionary project, and even though it was hard, I did. The next week I received some money I wasn't expecting, and it was the same amount that I gave away. The Lord returned what He had asked me to give!"

Most of us have probably heard testimonies like this. Nevertheless, it is always a challenge to grow in our giving patterns. But giving is clearly shown in the Word; in fact, it is a form of worship. As with everything else we have studied, God's purpose is not to diminish our lives in any way, but to bring us into full release. Let's study the offerings of worship and see how we can praise God in this vital part of our lives.

In this chapter we will look at the principle of giving and the scriptural basis of tithes and offerings. This study will help us learn how to give and to understand how giving brings release in all parts of our lives.

A principle of life

Giving is an integral part of worship. The offerings that are received at the churches we attend and our response to appeals for the needy are part of this, but there is more.

At the heart of the offering of worship is the offering of our lives. When Paul wrote to the Corinthians, he said,

> So I thought it necessary to urge the brothers to visit you in advance and finish the arrangements for the generous gift you had promised. Then it will be ready as a generous gift, not as one grudgingly given.

> Remember this: Whoever sows sparingly will also reap spar-
> ingly, and whoever sows generously will also reap generously.
> 2 Corinthians 9:5–6

Paul wasn't talking about any kind of reward that he might offer himself. He knew that the law of sowing and reaping is built into the fabric of life.

God has made us to be channels of His blessing. We can only be so when we allow Him to flow through us. He pours in and then He says, "Trust Me. Let go and more will come forth." More will come in direct proportion to our learning to release.

Worship, coming to know God's nature and worshiping Him with joy, begets a trust in the Lord and brings obedience. When we also follow that pathway of obedience in our giving, we manifest another aspect of worship.

When we give ourselves in worship, we are giving part of our lives. In the same way, when we give financially, we are giving of our lives. Almost everyone receives money according to an investment of part of their lives—usually in wages per hour or a monthly salary. What we are investing of our time and talents produces a monetary reward. So what we give of that represents our lives, ourselves.

Our attitude should be, "Lord, You are my life. You have made me what I am and given me the talents to do the work by which You provide for me. Because of Your faithfulness to me, I offer back a token of what I've already received from You." In offering back to God what He has given us, we are acknowledging that all of our life originates in Him. And we are opening ourselves up to a further flow of His resources to us.

A covenant for life

The Lord wants us to grow in learning His ways and His faithfulness. This learning includes the covenant of giving tithes and offerings. Most people accept the fact that they should give offerings, but tithing is more controversial. This is surprising, because tithing is clearly taught in Scripture and is endorsed by Jesus.

Tithing is part of a covenant for life established as early as the time of Abraham, before the Law was established. He paid tithes to Melchizedek, the priest of God Most High (Genesis 14). Abraham is commended throughout the New Testament as our example of faith. That means that we're not talking about legalism when we speak of tithes and offerings; we're dealing with the way of promise and faith.

There are always those who say, "Well, it's the Old Testament Law, and we've been freed from the Law." But I never hear people arguing that we should commit adultery and murder because we've been freed from the Law. They say, "That's different. Jesus spoke against murder and adultery." But Jesus endorsed tithing, too.

The Old Testament shows us what the covenant is all about. There is a dynamic principle of giving from the foundation of the tithe, from which we move on to faith-based offerings.

In Matthew 23:23 Jesus condemns the Pharisees because, while they are exacting and fussy about tithing, they have neglected the great matters of justice, mercy and faithfulness. He says, "You should have practiced the latter, without neglecting the former." In telling them this, Jesus is clearly saying that the tithe should not be neglected.

The New Testament case for giving is indisputable, even the principle of tithing. But if we focus too much on details, we are missing the point just as badly as the Pharisees did. God does not want us to split hairs in a legal debate. He wants ministry to flow through His Body to the whole world. The important matters of mercy, justice and faithfulness are still vital today, and God wants His people to make a difference in their cities, nations and beyond. That difference is made by prayer, giving and action.

Our message is more than a social gospel, but we cannot neglect the poor and suffering. Jesus would have us minister to them, and part of this ministry is by generous giving and responsible management. We begin to do this by giving tithes and offerings.

A presenting of life

Presenting our lives as an offering to the Lord doesn't always involve money. We also give ourselves. Paul said, "And now, brothers, we want you to know about the grace that God has given the Macedonian churches. Out of the most severe trial, their overflowing joy and their extreme poverty welled up in rich generosity. For I testify that they gave as much as they were able, and even beyond their ability. Entirely on their own, they urgently pleaded with us for the privilege of sharing in this service to the saints. And they did not do as we expected, but they gave themselves first to the Lord and then to us in keeping with God's will" (2 Corinthians 8:1–5). The people of the Macedonian church not only offered their support through money, but they offered themselves, first to the Lord and then to the service of the Church. Paul saw this as a great grace on their part, very much in keeping with God's will.

Jesus said, "If anyone gives even a cup of cold water to one of these little ones because he is my disciple, I tell you the truth, he will certainly be not lose his reward" (Matthew 10:42).

Let us recall again what Jesus said were the weightier matters of the Law: justice, mercy and faith. How do we attend to these matters? *Justice* relates to what is right, and we need to live in such a way that people see what is right by our actions. *Mercy* means that we help people with their problems even if they deserve what they got. These two virtues must go hand in hand. We can neither allow a legalistic sense of justice to go untempered by mercy nor let mercy become indulgent so that people have no opportunity to learn from the chastisement of justice. By *faith* we look to God to provide what is humanly impossible.

Finally, we are told, "Faith comes from hearing the message, and the message is heard through the word of Christ" (Romans 10:17). We are to offer ourselves by speaking the Word of God.

Giving of ourselves in service, helping people, caring and loving are all part of bringing offerings to the Lord. Let's never freeload on the abundance of God's kindness to us. Instead, let's be living examples of worship, offering all that we have and are.

Study questions:

1. How is giving an integral part of worship?
2. What is the law of sowing and reaping, and what does it mean for our lives?
3. What does the Bible teach about giving tithes and offerings?
4. In what way do we give ourselves, not just our money?
5. How is God challenging you now to worship Him in your giving?

12

The Fellowship of Worship

Since we began our study of worship, we have looked at the call of worship, the very God we worship, the beauty and the feast of worship. We've examined its meaning and fullness. We've looked also at songs of worship, the call to humility and the language of worship. We have considered the physical expressions of worship and the giving of our resources and our selves in worship.

Now we come to our life as brothers and sisters in Christ who worship Him. Coming together at a specific time and place focuses us in worship. The Lord has always brought His people together in fellowship.

In this chapter we will study the meaning of fellowship in worship. We will particularly focus on three essential elements of fellowship, with scriptural references for each one.

A time

The Bible directs us to have a time set apart to worship. Many excuse themselves from doing this regularly by saying, "I worship God all the time, in whatever I'm doing." That's good; everything we do should be glorifying to Him. But we also need regular times of concentrated worship with other believers.

In Exodus 20 God commanded the Israelites to remember the Sabbath and keep it holy. The New Testament clearly teaches that the issue is not which day of the week is observed, but that regular times of worship and fellowship are important.

Paul addresses this in Romans 14. There were apparently

different groups of Christians who had different opinions regarding the observance of a particular time. Paul said, "One man considers one day more sacred than another; another man considers every day alike. Each one should be fully convinced in his own mind. He who regards one day as special, does so to the Lord . . . . For none of us lives to himself alone . . . . Whether we live or die, we belong to the Lord" (Romans 14:5–8). The point is that we do everything for the Lord's sake.

However, lest anyone argue that it doesn't really matter if you observe a time of worship at all, we need to see the broader context of the New Testament. Although we are not taught that we need to observe a given day, we still need time set apart for the Lord. There must come a time when our bodies experience a reprieve and our souls are refreshed. God calls us to observe a day because *we* need it, both the physical rest and the spiritual renewal. So we are called to set aside a time to worship.

First Corinthians 16:2 says that the early Church gathered together on the first day of the week. Why that day? It was that day that Jesus rose from the dead, so Sunday became the Christian Sabbath. But even if that is difficult for you, keep a day to the Lord. There will be someplace and someone with whom you can worship on whichever day becomes your day to worship Him.

Hebrews 10:25 speaks these words to you and me: "Let us not give up meeting together, as some are in the habit of doing, but let us encourage one another—and all the more as you see the Day approaching."

A place

A place for worship has been a long tradition among the people of God. In the Old Testament, one of the first things that God did after bringing the Israelites out of Egypt was to direct them in establishing their patterns of worship. This included the building of the Tabernacle, which is written about in Exodus 25–31.

Several hundred years later, David desired to build a temple for the Lord. But God chose his son, Solomon, to build this great temple (1 Chronicles 17, 28). When the first contingent of Jews returned from Babylonian captivity, the first thing they did was rebuild the temple (Ezra 6).

Even when the Church was established, the practice of meeting at specific locations did not cease. In the earliest days of Christianity we are told that the believers continued to gather: "Every day they continued to meet together in the temple courts. They broke bread in their homes and ate together with glad and sincere hearts, praising God and enjoying the favor of all the people" (Acts 2:46–47). In Acts 20:20 we read that Paul taught groups of believers "publicly and from house to house."

There are those who think that Christians are more righteous if they function without buildings, but that misses the point. Buildings can be the death of a church, or they can be the center of its life. We are called together to worship, and we need a place in which to meet. By the time a local congregation grows to even seventy or eighty people, it is impractical to meet in a home. Just as you would seek larger housing to meet the needs of a growing family, so the family of God needs housing adequate to its size. The places may be great cathedrals or simple frame buildings, and they may be owned or rented, but they are centers for people to gather at a certain time to worship God.

A people

Finally, our fellowship inevitably involves people. There is a quality of joy when we gather together that is different from when we worship on our own. Meeting together strengthens those who are weak and encourages those who are struggling, so that all can grow in the life of faith.

The Bible teaches that there should be order in fellowship. In 1 Corinthians 16:15–16 and other epistles, Paul refers to people who were appointed leaders. In 1 Timothy and Titus we find that the leading elders were expected to meet a strict set of qualifications. This church government was initiated so that there would be accountability in the congregation, and a good order in the worship.

God honors our faithfulness in coming together and our

commitment to unity by bestowing the Holy Spirit on us. Psalm 133 says:

> How good and pleasant it is
> when brothers live together in unity!
> It is like precious oil poured on the head,
> running down on the beard,
> running down on Aaron's beard,
> down upon the collar of his robes.
> It is as if the dew of Hermon
> were falling on Mount Zion.
> For there the LORD bestows his blessing,
> even life forevermore.

When we gather together as one body, we see the release of His power. It is in worshiping that His power is released.

Just prior to His ascension, Jesus told the disciples to go to a mountain in Galilee. Once they had gathered, Jesus appeared to them, and when they saw Him, they worshiped Him. It was in that atmosphere of worship that Jesus said, "All authority in heaven and on earth has been given to me. Therefore go and make disciples of all nations, baptizing them in the name of the Father and of the Son and of the Holy Spirit, and teaching them to obey everything I have commanded you. And surely I am with you always, to the very end of the age" (Matthew 28:18–19).

To this day, where the Church comes together in worship, we receive the flow of Jesus' authority and His commission to go out and share all that we have already received. When we join in fellowship, we receive His power for the transforming of our world and the promise of His presence always.

And that's what worship is all about. May we live in that spirit.

Study questions:

1. What is the value of observing specific days or times for worship? Do you have a habit of setting aside particular times for the Lord?
2. How are places important for worship and fellowship?

3. What is unique about gathering together with other believers to worship?
4. What does God want to release when we worship Him together?
5. Are you living in the spirit of worship?

Jack Hayford is founding pastor of The Church on the Way in Van Nuys, California, and chancellor of The King's College and Seminary, an interdenominational ministry training center. He is the author of more than forty books and the host of a daily radio program and weekly television program, both of which are broadcast around the world by Living Way Ministries.